SPIRIT OF
CONNEMARA

RONAN BREE

First published in Great Britain in 2010

Copyright text and photographs © 2010 Ronan Bree

All rights reserved. No part of this publication may be reproduced, stored in a retrieval system, or transmitted in any form or by any means without the prior permission of the copyright holder.

British Library Cataloguing-in-Publication Data
A CIP record for this title is available from the British Library

ISBN 978 1 906887 74 2

PiXZ Books
Halsgrove House, Ryelands Industrial Estate,
Bagley Road, Wellington, Somerset TA21 9PZ UK
Tel: 00 44 1823 653777
Fax: 00 44 1823 216796
email: sales@halsgrove.com

An imprint of Halstar Ltd, part of the Halsgrove group of companies Information on all Halsgrove titles is available at: www.halsgrove.com

Printed and bound in China by Toppan Leefung Printing Ltd

Introduction

Connemara is the name given to the western portion of County Galway in Ireland, representing a vast open space found between Lough Corrib and the Atlantic Ocean. The unique wild landscape is decorated with mountain ranges, dotted with lakes, edged by an ocean with sandy shores and exists beneath a breathtaking, constantly changing, sky. Seasonally, Connemara practically changes colour allowing one to observe the spring and summer greens, the winter snow-capped mountains and even the autumnal shades of the land. The tranquil and serene aura combined with the spectacular natural beauty everywhere you look, makes Connemara the gateway to the heavens.

The colouring of
Connemara changes
seasonally, and at certain
times of year, green is
everywhere to be seen.

Opposite page:
Lough na Fooey is a
spectacular place, a glacial
lake surrounded by many
tall mountains. It even has
a sandy shoreline and is
well worth a visit.

Inagh Valley, the heart of Connemara.

Opposite page:
Lough na Fooey looks beautiful from a nearby vantage point.

Bog lanes can often be found decorating the landscape.

Opposite page: Dramatic sunsets are quite regular in Connemara. There are plenty of vantage points allowing you to observe the spectacular colours which decorate the sky.

The arches of the Quiet Man Bridge, show some detailed masonry.

Opposite page:
The view from the Quiet Man Bridge (as featured in 'The Quiet Man' movie). In this sunset shot, it almost appears as though God is lowering his foot through the clouds!

Derryclare Lake has a stunning island, sometimes referred to as Pine Island, that never fails to amaze. When the tide is low, you can walk out to the island on a small walkway. Leaving Connemara without seeing this island would mean you have to come back!

Opposite page:
A Quiet Man Bridge view on a sunny afternoon lets you appreciate the range of bright colours present.

The town of Roundstone prepares itself for a famous 'scattered shower',
a phrase which our weather forecasters often mention here in Ireland.
Opposite page:
A scenic view back to the Connemara mountain peaks from Roundstone,
a beautiful village with a lovely shoreline, in west Galway.

As the sun sets, the angle of the light is low and as you can see here, can illuminate any scene with beauty as well as with light.

Opposite page:
Ballynahinch allows a scenic viewpoint of the waterway beneath the peaks of the Connemara mountains, as the light suffuses the land.

Ballynahinch also possesses a small church with a graveyard which has some high cross gravestones that rise above the horizon reaching for the sky.

Opposite page: Close to Ballynahinch lake, is a sign for 'The Ranch' and behind the sign is this breathtaking view which shows how Connemara can fill a frame.

A dull day in Connemara does not mean a good photo is not obtainable.
This lake on the way to Maam from Maamcross was very still
providing a mirror image of the mountain in the reflection.
Opposite page:
Ballynahinch contains many spots for anglers as you can see here
with this small dock. They provide a real character to the view.

On the Clifden road from Leenane, there are spectacular vast open spaces full of colour. Here, an amazing cloud formation decorates the sky.

Opposite page: From the area around Leenane, you are able to look northwards towards Mayo. Killary harbour links this water to the Atlantic, but here you can see the calmness of the water as it had moved inland from the ocean.

Even though Connemara can appear deserted in spots, there are still fences dividing certain land. Here the natural Inagh Valley mountains tower above the man-made fence.

Opposite page:
Decorating the landscape are many small water features which act as mirrors on a calm day. Here this sheltered lake reflects the mountainous peak along Inagh Valley as the sun makes its way towards the horizon.

On the western side of Lough Inagh is a breath-taking and distinctive mountain range (The Twelve Pins [or Bens]).
Opposite page: Lough Inagh has plenty of places of beauty to photograph, however a nice cloud pattern can add to the scene on a still day. Inagh Lodge is evident on the horizon.

Facing west as the sun sets provides some brilliant scenes and colours.
Opposite page:
Pine Island of Derryclare Lake on a still day. I have only found this lake to be still once, and it provided me with the chance to capture its beauty twice (as it is and also in the reflection!).

The tall reeds of the lake's shoreline can provide some lovely foreground and colour to a scene.

Opposite page:
Just outside Oughterard, this waterlogged field adorns the roadside.

One of the many characters of Connemara. It always amazes me how calm these animals can be on the side of the road as cars whizz past.

Opposite page:
As you enter Connemara, you quickly notice how the landscape 'opens up'.
No better example than this lake which meets you before Maamcross
and provides a lovely scene.

Here, the sun can be fleetingly seen behind a cloud. In the forgeground is a rock mass present at the side of Lough Inagh.

Saving the turf is evident throughout Connemara. The large stack piled here should provide heat for an Irish winter.

Cattle graze on grass land beneath Derryclare moutain on a cloudy day.

Opposite page: On the way back to Galway via the south coast of the county (which eventually leads you through Spiddal) is this wonderful scene. A long narrow lake rests at the foot of this giant mountainous landscape.

A Connemara horse poses nicely for a photo.

Opposite page:
The rugged shoreline of Lough Inagh decorates the foreground on a gloomy day in Connemara.

Even on an overcast day, a patch of blue sky appears.

Opposite page: The underwater reeds in this stream move with the flow of the water.

The split branches stretch and reach for the heavens.

Opposite page:
A cloud formation rests comfortably between the
peaks of the Connemara mountains.

The water zig zags its way down through Inagh Valley.

Opposite page: The sun comes down over Derryclare Lake.

The low angle of light on a winter's afternoon illuminates a north Connemara scene.

Opposite page: Inagh Valley woodlands show the light at the end of the tunnel.

Just outside Clifden
lies a superb coral
shoreline, with its almost
fluorescent green water.
A joy to visit for a stroll.

Opposite page:
As you make your way
towards Maam from
Maamcross, this stunning
lake grabs your attention
surrounded by mountains
and reeds under an
atmospheric sky.

I usually drive through Connemara with my windows down keeping my ears pricked for the sound of flowing water. Such a trick, brought me across this scene on the way to Leenane.

Opposite page:
Before you reach Maam, this scene will grab your attention, where you can see layer upon layer of mountains in the distance.

This mountain range appears golden from the sunlight being cast on it.

Opposite page: A view looking back up through Killary harbour towards Lennane.

A mountainous landscape towers about Lough Inagh.

Opposite page: The inviting road down to Inagh Valley is well worth taking.

When you walk out to Derryclare Island (when the tide is low and you can take the small path out), the tall trees on the island provide beauty from every angle.

Opposite page:
Facing north up Lough Inagh can give some wonderful scenes.

A Roundstone boat takes some rest on dry land.

Opposite page:
A branched view up towards Ballynahinch Castle which is evident nestled in the trees.

A shy horse hides behind some Connemara gorse.

Opposite page:
This golden-haired horse was guarding his patch on a Connemara mountain.

The local wildlife can act as great models for a photoshoot!

Opposite page: Ballynahinch Lake is the home of beautiful sunsets as can be seen here, where a golden, orange sky grabs the attention.

Kylemore Abbey, always a popular spot in Connemara,
is well worth a visit, as it towers over a still lake.